Coming of Age

Mandy Ross

Heinemann
LIBRARY

www.heinemann.co.uk/library

Visit our website to find out more information about **Heinemann Library** books.

To order:

 Phone 44 (0) 1865 888066

 Send a fax to 44 (0) 1865 314091

Visit the Heinemann Bookshop at www.heinemann.co.uk/library to browse our catalogue and order online.

First published in Great Britain by Heinemann Library, Halley Court, Jordan Hill, Oxford OX2 8EJ, part of Harcourt Education. Heinemann is a registered trademark of Harcourt Education Ltd.

© Harcourt Education Ltd 2003
The moral right of the proprietor has been asserted.

Editorial: Jilly Attwood and Claire Throp
Design: David Poole and Geoff Ward
Picture Research: Rosie Garai and Su Alexander
Production: Séverine Ribierre

Originated by Ambassador Litho Ltd
Printed in Hong Kong by Wing King Tong

ISBN 0 431 17711 2
07 06 05 04 03
10 9 8 7 6 5 4 3 2 1

British Library Cataloguing in Publication Data
Ross, Mandy
Coming of Age - (Rites of Passage)
392.1'4
A full catalogue record for this book is available from the British Library.

Acknowledgements
The publishers would like to thank the following for permission to reproduce photographs:
Andes Press Agency pp. **15**, **19**; Ann & Bury Peerless p. **20**; AP p. **7** (David Arnston); Christine Osbourne p. **21**; Circa p. **27** (Christine Osbourne); Corbis pp. **6** (Jonathan Blair), **10** (Chris Lisle), **16** (Penny Tweedie), **23** (Patrick Ward), **26** (Hulton-Deutsch Collection), **29** (Chuck Savage); Getty Images p. **5** (David Young-Wolff); Hutchison Picture Library p. **13**; Images of Africa p. **4**; Impact pp. **8**, **9** (Piers Cavendish), **24** (Tadashi Kajiyama); Israelimages.com p. **18** (Yasha Mazur); Link p. **12** (Adrian Arbib); Lonely Planet Images pp. **17** (Richard I'Anson), **25** (Bill Wassman); Magnum Photos p. **11** (Abbas); North Wind Picture Archives p. **14**; Popperfoto/Reuters p. **28**; South American Pictures p. **22**

Cover photograph of Masai boys wearing ceremonial clothing after ritual circumcision, reproduced with permission of Corbis/Ralph A. Clevenger.

The publishers would like to thank both the Interfaith Education Centre, Bradford and Georga Godwin for their assistance in the preparation of this book.

Every effort has been made to contact copyright holders of any material reproduced in this book. Any omissions will be rectified in subsequent printings if notice is given to the publishers.

Contents

Any words printed in bold letters, **like these**,
are explained in the Glossary.

What are rites of passage?

As we get older, each of us goes through important life changes, such as growing from childhood into adulthood, marrying, having children, and dying.

All around the world, people gather together to mark these changes for friends and relatives in their community. Often they carry out **rituals**, such as prayers or special actions, or celebrate with dancing or a party. These rituals or celebrations are called rites of passage.

Coming of age

This book explores some rites of passage that mark the time when a child becomes an adult, called 'coming of age'. The book is organized in order of the age when each rite of passage usually takes place.

These boys from the Maasai in Tanzania are wearing special clothing as part of their coming-of-age ceremony.

There are many different ways of celebrating coming of age. Some are religious **ceremonies**, welcoming the young person as a new adult member of the faith. Others are based on day-to-day life – for instance, starting to teach young people things they will need to know as adults, such as work skills or how to provide food.

At a coming-of-age ceremony, a child is starting to leave behind the world of childhood, and taking a step towards a new stage of life as a young adult. He or she is getting ready to join a new group – the adult world.

Coming of age is celebrated some time between the ages of 12 and 21. This girl is celebrating her eighteenth birthday. Many cultures believe that eighteen is the age when a child becomes an adult.

Rites of passage

In 1909, a man called Arnold van Gennep wrote about rites of passage, which mark important moments of change in a person's life. He said there are three changes in every rite of passage:

• leaving one group
• moving on to a new stage
• and joining a new group.

Holy Communion and confirmation

Holy Communion is when **Christians** remember the Last Supper, the meal shared by Jesus and his disciples on the day before he died. Many **Roman Catholic** children celebrate their first Holy Communion at the age of seven. Special prayers are said and each person is given a wafer or piece of bread and a sip of wine.

Girls and boys take their First Communion together. Girls often wear a white dress, while boys dress in a shirt and tie. In some ways, the **ceremony** is like a wedding. The children are promising themselves to Jesus, and promising to live as good Christians. The ceremony **symbolizes** that they are now full members of the Christian church.

Roman Catholic boys and girls after their First Communion.

Confirmation

In the Roman Catholic, **Methodist** and **Anglican** churches, young people may be confirmed. This usually happens between the ages of twelve and sixteen, when they are considered old enough to understand Christianity and choose to be a Christian. They are confirming their parents' and godparents' promises (made at their **christening** or **baptism**) to bring them up as Christians.

Teenagers preparing for their confirmation in the USA. At their confirmation they will promise to follow the teachings of Jesus Christ.

Melanie's story

Melanie, a Catholic, remembers her First Communion:

'I went to classes to prepare for First Communion. We read stories from the Bible and learnt about Jesus' life. On the day of my First Communion, I loved dressing up, having my hair done and wearing new shoes with silver buckles on! But I remember it was a serious and special day. I was given my own little prayer book, so that I could say my prayers along with the adults.'

Entering a Buddhist monastery

In countries such as Vietnam, Thailand and Burma, most of the people are **Buddhists**. In Buddhist countries, young boys may spend some months or years in Buddhist **monasteries** to learn more about Buddhism. In countries like Thailand, almost every boy does this. Girls can enter a Buddhist **nunnery** for some time, too, although fewer girls do so.

Boys can enter a monastery at any age. Most boys wait until they are about eight or ten years old. The boy's head is shaved to **symbolize** a fresh start. He wears simple orange robes, like the other **monks**. His daily life is just like that of a grown-up monk. He helps with jobs such as cooking or cleaning, and has lessons in Buddhism and other ordinary school subjects. After his time in the monastery, the boy returns to live with his family, to work or continue with his education.

Young boys living as monks in a Buddhist monastery in Thailand.

Young boys in a procession to enter a monastery in Burma.

In Burma, there is a special **ceremony** for a boy entering a monastery. He leaves his home wearing his finest clothes, riding on horseback. This is a symbol of the Buddha, a prince who went out from his palace to search for understanding. Then when the boy reaches the monastery, he takes off his fine clothes, as a symbol that the Buddha left behind his life as a prince to teach about Buddhism. Instead the boy will wear the simple robes of a monk.

Muslim Hatum ceremony

Every day after school, many **Muslim** children go to classes at their mosque, the Muslim place of worship. They start some time between the ages of five and seven years old.

At the mosque they learn about Islam (the religion of Muslims) and the Qur'an (say 'kor-ARN'), the Muslim **holy** book. Each day, they read a few verses of the Qur'an. After they have been going for two or three years, they may be ready for their Hatum **ceremony**. This ceremony marks the time when someone has read the whole of the Qur'an from beginning to end.

These children are at a class in the mosque. They are learning to read the Qur'an.

Fasting at Ramadan

Another sign of growing up comes during the Muslim month of Ramadan. During Ramadan, adult Muslims fast during the hours of daylight. This means they do not eat or drink anything from sunrise to sunset. From the age of seven, Muslim children may start by fasting for just a few days each Ramadan. Gradually they fast for more days each year, until by the age of twelve, they are expected to fast just like the adults throughout the month.

This girl is learning the Qur'an by heart.

Farrah's story

Farrah Rehman is a Muslim girl from Birmingham, UK. Here, she remembers her Hatum ceremony:

'When I was ten years old, I was ready for my Hatum. I felt really nervous, even though I'd been practising. My mum came with my sister and nieces and nephews. I read aloud the last ten surah, or verses, of the Qur'an. All my class listened as I read. I did make a few little mistakes, but my teacher sat with me, and she corrected me. When I finished, everyone said, "Marsh'allah!", which means "Well done!" We brought sweets and rice for everyone in my class. I felt so happy that I'd finished reading the Qur'an.'

11

African initiation ceremonies

In many ancient, traditional cultures, **initiation ceremonies** mark the time when a child enters the adult world. Often this is at the time of **puberty** – that is, when girls' and boys' bodies change as they become adults.

Boys eating bull fat as part of their initiation ceremony in Kenya, east Africa.

Haggai's story

Haggai remembers his initiation ceremony in Kenya when he was fourteen:

'*Before the ceremony began, we built a hut in the forest far from our village. The women sang to encourage us to be strong and brave. Then all the men of the tribe gathered to watch our **circumcision**. It was very painful, but bearing the pain shows that you are a man.*

'*We lived in the hut for three months. Elders from our tribe taught us skills we would need as adults, such as hunting for food. Afterwards, we were welcomed back into our tribe as men. I looked forward to my initiation, even though I knew it would be hard, because I was ready to become a man.*'

There are many different initiation ceremonies across Africa. Most of them are to emphasize that at puberty, boys and girls are starting to leave their childhood and their family behind. Instead they are becoming part of the adult community.

Girls' initiation rites

There are different initiation rites for girls. In parts of Zambia, in southern Africa, a ceremony called 'dancing the chisungu' marks a girl's coming of age. The headman of the tribe blesses the girl by calling to the spirits of beloved **ancestors**. Then each day for several weeks, the girl performs **ritual** dances. These dances **symbolize** traditional ways of catching fish, making clay pots, and other skills that she will need as a grown woman.

A girl at her initiation ceremony in Sierra Leone, west Africa.

Native American sunrise ceremony

When the Europeans arrived in North America in the 17th century, many Native American customs were no longer allowed. But today Native American families in the USA are reviving some of the ancient **rituals**.

Many girls of the Apache (say 'a-PATCH-ee') tribe, in south-western USA, have a four-day coming-of-age ritual. The ritual is called the sunrise **ceremony**. It is held in the summer after the girl's first **menstrual period**.

The family chooses a godmother for the girl. The godmother will have a special relationship with the girl throughout her life. Before sunset, the godmother dresses the girl in special animal-skin robes decorated with feathers, beads and shells. At this time, the girl is believed to have special healing powers.

Many Native American ceremonies and gatherings were banned by the new European settlers.

Changing Woman

The sunrise ceremony acts out the Native American **myth** of the first woman, known as Changing Woman. The myth tells how she survived the great flood, and gave birth to two sons. When she grows old, Changing Woman walks east towards the sun until she meets her younger self, and she becomes young again. Each girl dances the part of Changing Woman during her sunrise ceremony. In this way, according to the myth, Changing Woman becomes a part of every new **generation** of young women.

At her sunrise ceremony the girl must dance for up to six hours through each day and each night. This is a very long, hard test of the girl's strength. Her godmother dances with the girl to help her.

By the end of the ceremony, many girls feel proud of their strength and how long they danced for. They feel ready to start taking on adult responsibilities.

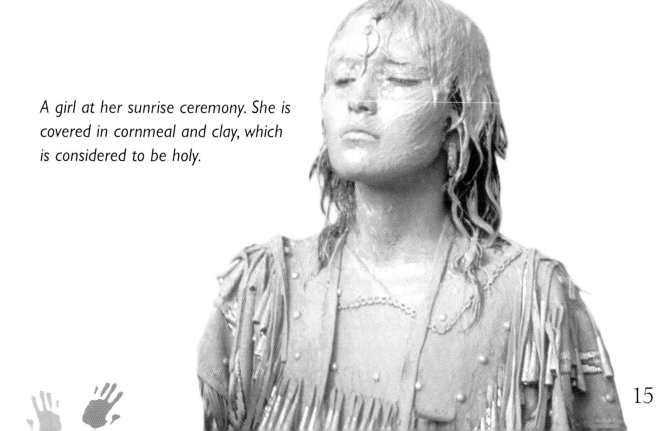

A girl at her sunrise ceremony. She is covered in cornmeal and clay, which is considered to be holy.

Aboriginal puberty rituals

Many Aboriginal peoples in Australia hold **rituals** at **puberty**, to prepare boys for manhood. The Walbiri people of central Australia hold a ritual for groups of up to fifteen boys.

The elders of the tribe decide exactly when the boys are ready, usually between the ages of eleven and thirteen. The boys go to live for a while in the 'bush', the wild and dry landscape of inner Australia. They are leaving their childhood world behind them, living apart from their parents and families.

The boys' bodies are painted with ochre, a natural red or yellow dye. The leader of the clan leads the boys in dances. The elders of the tribe tell the ancient stories of the Dreamtime, the Aboriginal time of **myth**. These stories teach about practical tasks, such as hunting, and the use of herbs for healing. The stories also teach about how society should be organized.

An Aboriginal boy preparing for his initiation ceremony.

The most important part of the **initiation ceremony** is **circumcision**. This is a painful ritual, but it is important for the Walbiri people that the boys go through the pain. Shedding blood **symbolizes** the 'death' of childhood, as the young men are 'reborn' into the world of manhood.

So the initiation ceremony happens for two reasons: it brings young boys into manhood, and it preserves the traditions and stories of Aboriginal clans.

A girl grinding stone into powder. The powder will be used to make traditional Aboriginal art.

Learning about Aboriginal art

Aboriginal paintings, made out of natural materials, such as bark and vegetable dyes, also tell the stories of the Dreamtime. Many Aboriginal artists are women. When their daughters are growing up, these artists teach them how to paint the traditional paintings of their clan or family, so that they can keep the traditions alive.

Jewish Bar and Bat Mitzvah

When a **Jewish** boy is thirteen, he can become Bar Mitzvah to mark the beginning of being a grown-up. In many synagogues (Jewish place of worship), Jewish girls become Bat Mitzvah when they are twelve or thirteen. In some Orthodox (strictly traditional) synagogues a number of girls share a Bat Chayil celebration instead.

Most Bar and Bat Mitzvah **ceremonies** take place in the synagogue. Usually, the ceremony forms part of the weekly service on Saturday morning. The young person is called up to the front of the synagogue. Then he or she reads aloud from the Torah, the Jewish **holy** book. The Torah is written in Hebrew, the language of Judaism, on a scroll (roll of paper).

This Israeli boy is carrying the Torah before his Bar Mitzvah ceremony at the Western Wall, Jerusalem. This is a very important place in the history of Judaism.

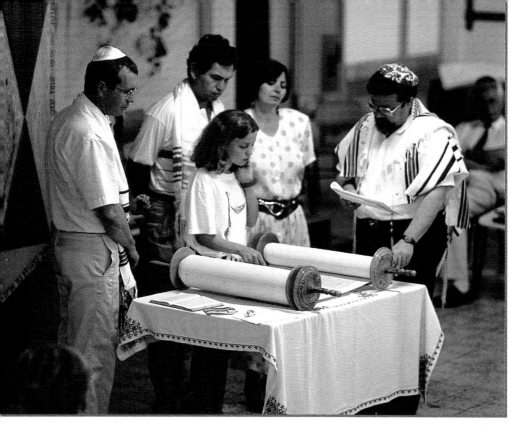

A Bat Mizvah celebration in a synagogue.

After the service, there is often a party for family and friends to celebrate this important day. After they have become Bar or Bat Mitzvah, young people are considered to be young adults within the synagogue and the Jewish community. They are encouraged to take an adult role in the synagogue.

Sarah's story

Sarah, a Jewish girl, remembers her Bat Mitzvah, when she was thirteen years old:

'All my family and friends came to our synagogue on the day of my Bat Mitzvah ceremony. I had been studying for several months beforehand. At first, I felt very nervous. But once I started reading from the Torah scroll, I forgot my nerves.

'Afterwards, everyone congratulated me and we had a great party! Over the months that followed, I started to be treated like an adult in the synagogue, and I began to teach the younger children at Sunday school.'

Hindu Upanayana ceremony

There are sixteen different ceremonies that take place during a Hindu's life. These are called samskars and they mark a change in a person's life. The tenth samskar is the Upanayama, or sacred thread, ceremony. It takes place when a Hindu boy is aged between eight and twelve, and is the time when he becomes a member of the Hindu religion. Only boys from certain castes (social classes) can take part.

At the ceremony, the boy's head is shaved and he puts on a simple cotton wrap. Then he is given a sacred thread and told, 'Now you are a man.' The boy then recites the Gyatri Mantra (a famous hymn from the Vedas, the oldest of the Hindu **holy** books). The sacred thread is a loop with three strands of strong cotton. The three strands **symbolize** three important forms of God (Brahman): Brahma, Vishnu and Shiva. The boy wears the thread looped over his left shoulder and across his chest. He will wear the thread for the rest of his life. After the ceremony, there is a big party for friends and family.

A boy wearing the sacred thread at his Upanayana ceremony.

Hinduism is the main religion in India. Hindus believe in Brahman, the supreme God. Hindus believe that the supreme God cannot be described or imagined in any way. So, to help them understand Brahman they worship the supreme God through gods and goddesses. They see Brahman in three roles – as a creator, a preserver and a destroyer. Brahma is the creator of life while Vishnu keeps life going (preserves life). Shiva is the part of the supreme God responsible for the death of living things.

This statue is of the Hindu god Brahman.

Hindus also believe that there has to be both male and female parts to the supreme god. This means that goddesses are also important in Hinduism. The female is often the opposite of the male. If the god is harsh then the goddess will be kind. There is a Mother Goddess who can be worshipped in different forms. She can be seen as Durga or Kali, and is also Shiva's wife, Parvati.

Quinceañera

In many Latin American countries, such as Cuba and Mexico, girls celebrate their Quinceañera (say 'KWIN-chay-a-NYAIR-a') on their fifteenth birthday. Sometimes it is called the Quince or Quince Anos. This is seen as the start of being a woman. Traditionally, after her Quinceañera, a girl was seen as being ready to marry – although today, many girls prefer to wait until they have finished their education before getting married.

The Quinceañera is often celebrated in the USA, too, especially among Hispanic families who originally came from Latin American countries.

Family and friends gather for a Quinceañera celebration in Mexico.

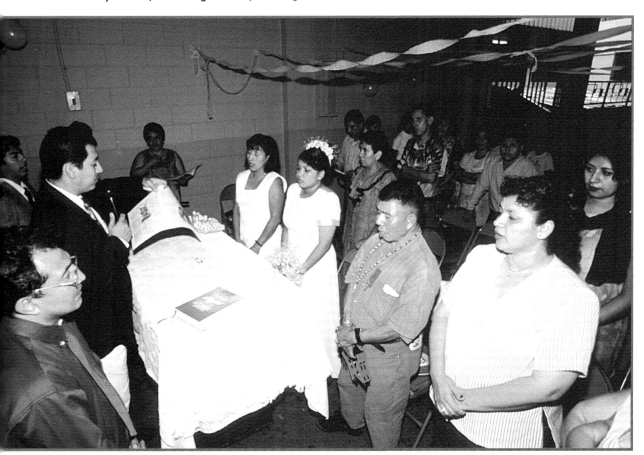

A father taking his daughter to her Quinceañera party.

Traditionally, the Quinceañera is a very elaborate and splendid party, quite like a wedding. Families may save up money for many years to give their daughters a memorable party. The girl chooses a gown in white or pastel shades. A hairdresser comes to do her hair. On the day itself there may be a short service in church, but the celebration is mainly a non-religious, family gathering. The girl's mother crowns her with a jewelled tiara. Her father takes away her satin slippers, a **symbol** of childhood, and gives her instead a pair of woman's high-heeled shoes.

Some girls are offered the choice between a Quinceañera celebration or their first car. By choosing the Quinceañera a Latin-American girl maintains her cultural traditions and celebrates her heritage.

Japanese Coming-of-Age Day

In Japan, Seijin No Hi or Coming-of-Age Day is a national holiday celebrated every January. It marks the coming of age of every young man and woman who has reached their twentieth birthday that year.

Young men wear a new suit for the special day. Young women dress in traditional, brightly-coloured kimonos called furisode (say 'foo-ree-soh-deh'). Celebrations are organized by local governments, schools or businesses. There may be speeches by important local people, congratulating the young people on becoming adults. They are given a special gift to remember the day, and they promise to become responsible members of society. After the **ceremony** they may visit temples or shrines, or celebrate in town with their friends.

Young Japanese women wearing beautiful kimonos for their Coming-of-Age Day.

Seijin No Hi is a bright and spectacular sight on a winter's day each year. The ceremony goes back to the 8th century. Then, young boys from powerful families took on adult clothing and hairstyles. Coming-of-Age Day was made a national holiday by law in 1948. It helped to build up people's spirits as Japan was recovering after World War II.

Coming of age in Korea

Korea also has a Coming-of-Age Day, on the third Monday in May. Boys' long hair is tied into a top knot and they are given a kat, a traditional Korean hat made of horsehair. Girls have their hair put up and secured with an ornamental hairpin called a pinyo. There are great celebrations for family and friends.

This photograph shows a Korean girl wearing a pinyo, a special hairpin, in a traditional hairstyle on Coming-of-Age day.

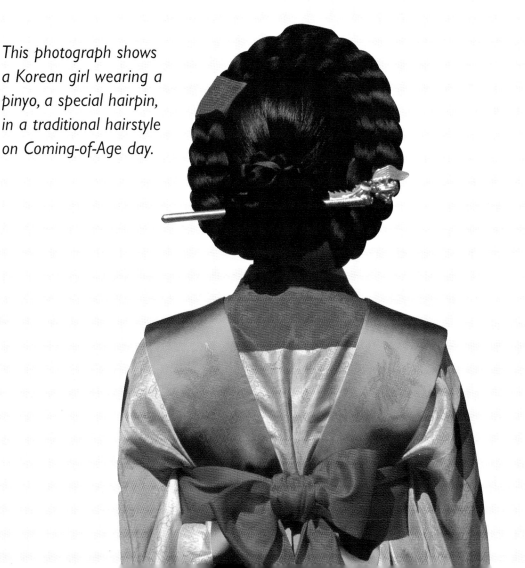

New rituals from old

In the past, many young people marked the change from childhood to adulthood within their religion. Others marked it by starting work. Young men often learnt their trade as an apprentice, a kind of trainee. An older man would teach the apprentice boy the skills he would need, guiding him into the new world of work.

But these traditions are no longer common in the developed world. Many people follow no religion, and young people may continue in education long after their bodies are grown up. Some families are starting to recognize the need for new **rituals** to mark the change from childhood to adulthood.

A young apprentice learning engineering at a school in Manchester, UK.

Some people are making new rituals, often taking ideas from Aboriginal and African **initiation** rites. Fathers may take their sons into the forest for a camping trip when they reach **puberty**. The men's movement in the USA is developing new rituals for men and boys, such as drumming and chanting together, and learning survival skills in the wild. These rituals help boys to learn about becoming men. They also help boys to develop bonds with older men, so that they feel a part of a male family of **generations**.

This young Christian woman is reading a prayer.

New religious rituals

Some women are seeking rituals for girls' life events that conventional religion has ignored — for instance, the start of their **menstrual periods**. **Jewish** and **Christian** woman have written new prayers and adapted traditional ones to mark this time. They are celebrating the moment when a girl's body becomes a woman's, enabling her to become a mother in the future.

Growing up, moving on

In many countries in the West, including the UK, Australia and the USA, many people no longer belong to religious organizations such as the church. So, many young people mark their coming of age, or growing up, in a non-religious way, with a special birthday party when they are 18 or 21. This marks the beginning of adulthood.

For many young people, leaving home is an important move towards adulthood. Some leave home to go to college or university. Others leave home when they are working and can afford to pay their own rent. Many young people start by sharing a flat with a few friends. Then they have to do their own shopping, laundry and housework, cook their own meals, and decide for themselves when to go to bed, get up, study and go out.

A French teenager voting in her first election.
Voting is an important right for young adults.

The start of adulthood is an exciting time. Some young adults feel a mixture of happiness and sadness at leaving behind their childhood. Becoming an adult brings new responsibilities – but it can also bring new beginnings and new freedoms.

Rights by law

In each country, the law gives new rights to people when they reach adulthood. They are allowed to do things that children cannot do, for instance, vote, learn to drive, or get married without their parents' consent. Once a person has reached the age of adulthood, they can decide for themselves. The age when the law allows each of these things varies from country to country, but usually it is some time between fifteen and eighteen.

Students meeting friends outside their college.

Glossary

ancestor relative in the past. Your grandparents and great-grandparents are your ancestors.

Anglicans people who belong to a branch of Protestantism including the Church of England

baptism when someone is welcomed into Christianity

Buddhists (Buddhism) people who follow the way of life taught by the Buddha, who lived in ancient India about 2500 years ago. The Buddha was not a god, but a man. He taught his followers how to live simple, peaceful lives.

ceremony a special ritual and celebration

christening when a baby or child is welcomed into Christianity and their name is blessed

Christians (Christianity) people who follow the religion of Christianity, which is based on the teachings of Jesus Christ. Christians believe that Jesus was the Son of God.

circumcise (circumcision) cut away the foreskin, the skin that covers the tip of the penis

generation all the people born around the same time

Hindus (Hinduism) people who follow Hinduism. Hindus worship one god (called Brahman) in many forms. Hinduism is the main religion in India.

holy special because it is to do with God or a religious purpose

initiation bringing someone into a new group or community

Jews (Judaism) people who follow the religion of Judaism. Jews pray to one god. Their holy book is the Hebrew Bible, sometimes called the Old Testament by Christians.

menstrual period monthly bleeding that starts when a girl reaches puberty

Methodists people who belong to a branch of Christianity that began in the 18th century

monastery all-male religious community

monk member of a monastery, an all-male religious community. Monks devote their lives to God.

Muslims (Islam) people who follow the religion of Islam. Muslims pray to one god, whom they call Allah.

myth a traditional story, often about supernatural beings, and sometimes used to explain why natural events have happened

nunnery all-female religious community

Protestants people who believe in a form of Christianity that began in Germany in the 16th century, when Christians first broke away from the Pope's leadership

puberty when a girl's or boy's body changes into an adult's

Roman Catholics Christians who follow the leadership of the Pope in Rome

sacred another word for holy

secular not following any religion

Sikhs (Sikhism) people who follow the religion of Sikhism, based on the teachings of the ten Gurus, or teachers

symbol/symbolize when a picture, object or action stands for something else

Further resources

More books to read

Celebrations (series), Anita Ganeri (Heinemann Library, 2001)

Religions of the World (series), Sue Penney (Heinemann Library, 2002)

Index

Titles in the *Rites of Passage* series include:

Hardback   0 431 17715 5

Hardback   0 431 17711 2

Hardback   0 431 17712 0

Hardback   0 431 17713 9

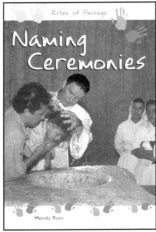

Hardback   0 431 17710 4

Hardback   0 431 17714 7

Find out about the other titles in this series on our website www.heinemann.co.uk/library